Thoughts
anxious soul

Harry Nixon

Thoughts from an anxious soul © 2023
Harry Nixon

All rights reserved.

No part of this publication may be reproduced, stored in a retrieval system, or transmitted, in any form or by any means, electronic, mechanical, photocopying, recording or otherwise, without the prior written permission of the presenters.

Harry Nixon asserts the moral right to be identified as author of this work.

Presentation by *BookLeaf Publishing*

Web: www.bookleafpub.com

E-mail: info@bookleafpub.com

ISBN: 9789357216159

First edition 2023

ACKNOWLEDGEMENT

To my Mum, Dad, and siblings, Stephanie, Jack, Jessica and George, thank you for the love and support shown to me, the guidance and the many life lessons learnt.

To Rosie and Sebastian for being little balls of inspirations and Auntie Maz for being a confidant and a person always a call away during my times of crisis.

PREFACE

During the pandemic, I became restless and bored, itching for the next big adventure. I started writing little passages, hoping something would come of them, but nothing came of it. Now, I am throwing myself into my writing, day by day, week by week and pushing my overly anxious self, out of my comfort zone and into the unknown ready to explore this unchartered territory.

Brave me

Brave me, strong me,
A year has passed, and I am still me,
A new chapter upon me, and I feel ready,
Positivity I will embrace, kindness I will reap,
I deserve this, let's do this, together,
Speak soon and take care, me.

Why do I feel like this?

Why do I feel like this?
Completely empty, depleted, and on the verge of defeat…
Thoughts so loud I cannot process, what is happening to me?
The walls are closing in, the water is rising, and the sky is falling beside me.
How dare they!
How dare I!
I'll be fine, promise,
Don't worry about me... I'll be fine... promise...

Jack, my twin

Jack,
My best friend, my soul mate,
Born together, identical twins,
I am glad were twins, you understand me
You keep me sane, even if the odds are against us,
Brilliant Jack, don't change, the world is full of sheep,
I love you, Jack

The Singer and I

The Singer and I
Best of friends, against the world,
Creative, passionate, and lost souls, in a confusing world,
Singer, an angel in a human form with a human soul,
She looks after me, as do I look after her,
A different type of soul mate, a platonic soul mate, lifelong soul mate.
Sing the friendship song, Singer, for it is us against the world,
The Singer and I

Help me

Help me,
I have done it again.
Self-pity and self-disgust are eating at me…
Do I need help, or is this for attention?
Am I allowed to feel like this?
Sleepless nights, I feel more alive
I hope one day, I will learn to value myself
Love myself more and be more kind to myself,
Bear with me, I am learning to help myself now..

A bumpy ride

Anxiety is a bitch,
Fake love is fake, and I feel so low.
The world will continue to orbit, and I have vertigo,
Help me, I feel like I am dying here.
The beach is calm, the waves are ferocious,
I feel sick, help me, I don't like this ride.
Make it stop, I cannot do this anymore...
Another lost, and anxious soul calls this life,
Is life one big test, a sick social experiment?
Hold on tight, for this is going to be a bumpy ride.
A rollercoaster of emotions,
Fake love, real love, what's real what's not?
Different anxieties, different scenarios
Different people, different experiences,
Like I said, this is going to be a bumpy ride.

Little man, Sebastian

Little man, Sebastian
A precious treasure of mine,
A ray of sunshine, and a bundle of joy,
Little man, Sebastian
A smile so bright it brightens the room,
A personality of love that feeds the soul,
I love my favourite little man,
Creative, inspirational and amazing,
Dream as big as your personality,
Stand with your head held high,
I am always with you, Sebastian,
Life is a journey, I hope to be a part of,
But for now Sebastian,
Be good, continue to be great,
My little man, Sebastian

Mr. Darcy, our beloved beast

Mr. Darcy, our beloved cat
Our loss of you seems unbearable,
Our pain and grief seem to last forever,
The loss of you, Mr. Darcy, is unimaginable,
I hear you, sing in the halls early in the morning,
The pitta patter when you walk around the house,
The comfort you brought to me when I needed comfort,
You showed e a different kind of love,
And when I needed a hand I found a paw, Your paw,
Mr. Darcy,
RIP, Mr. Darcy, you immortalized beast,
Forever in my heart and the hearts of the family,
Long live, Mr. Darcy, our beloved beast.

Why me?

Why me?
What did I possess that someone else in the same place didn't?
What made me your target of such hatred and cruelty?
I didn't even know you then, now I am scarred for life of a memory
A memory of such violence and hostility, I cannot control my own self.
HOW DARE YOU!
Taken something from me that you shouldn't have taken,
A piece of me I will never get back, a memory engraved into my DNA.
I am trying to forget, but PTSD is killing me,
I survived, and for now, I am just living a half-emptied life.
Smile more, be kinder to yourself, are things I hear a lot of,
What makes me different now is that I am a survivor
A badge of honour I didn't want to wear
You will not see me fall apart, you won't see my fall and lose my crown,
I am surviving, the best I can,
I have faith in myself, the universe, my friends and family,
I believe in me.

My beloved friend

My beloved friend, why did you leave me?
We were best of friends, was we not?
What happened to us, to make you do what you did?
I miss you… I'll miss you dearly.
Life was hard for you, and has been difficult for me too,
I hope you are well my friend; I miss you.
One day, we will meet again, but for now take care,
My beloved friend, I miss you

Sleepless nights

Sleepless nights, I lay awake with my demons,
I have made peace with them, and they have become a comfort,
I lay awake wondering, why is living a life becoming more of a nightmare?
Life should be fun, exciting, loving, but instead is pain, suffering, and horrors
I close my eyes, hoping to drift, like a boat in the sea approaching a storm,
I remember everything, feel everything, and more…
Yet I know that I must continue to live my life and keep my demons at bay
And hope that one day, a good nights sleep is what I get.

The Balance

The children play, the adults play
2 different games, 2 different outcomes,
One game full of innocence, kindness and love
The other game full of, pain, suffering and hatred.
Why do we play these games with ourselves?
Life is a weighing scale, both sides to create an equal balance
Where there is good, there is evil, there is no middle ground
Us humans, we are the spectrum of good and evil, and the shades between,
As the world continues its orbit, as do our lives.

Our Cries

A mothers cry, and the world revolts,
People demand justice, but where from?
A fathers cry, and the aggression takes over,
Violence ensues, danger is all around.
Why would they do such a thing
Why is no one helping them,
Cries for help get louder, the world mourns,
The innocence we once knew, taken forcefully.
We want justice, WE WANT JUSTICE!
The cries are louder, and more ferocious,
The world is intense, my anxiety is high,
Why is no one helping us, can anyone hear our cries?

Calm before the storm

The calm before the storm is the worst,
The build-up of anxiety cripples me,
I can hear the waves crashing, the thunderstorm, the torrential winds,
It excites me, I know I can weather the storm, and survive it,
Something about calm freaks me out, I cannot put my finger on it,
Maybe I am being controlled and ruled by my anxiety,
Maybe I enjoy the thrill and the excitement a storm can bring,
The waves crashing across the calm sands on a beach,
The chill of the open aired winds around the beach,
The calm before the storm is awful, but I know that I will be fine in the storm,
I know that I will be fine

Rosie

My beloved cousin, Rosie,
Such a beauty, your humour, and presence fill the world
Oh, how I enjoy our conversations,
My beloved cousin, Rosie,
How independent and head strong you are,
An infectious personality, an infectious smile,
Not a sheep, but a shepherd you are,
You will inspire change, you will reshape the world,
Don't change for society, Rosie,
You're a force to be reckoned with,
My dearest beloved cousin, Rosie, I love you

Mother

Mother, you are strong,
You inspire and grace me every day,
You fight for your beliefs, and stand in your truths,
Oh, I wish I had your strength, Mother.
Your compassion and kindness often go unnoticed,
But I always notice, I want to be kinder and more compassionate,
Mother, help me, guide me, I need some guidance,
I love you forever and a day, Mother.
God bless, Mother, your son, Harry.

Hurts

My heart hurts,
It feels as if it has been ripped in two,
Every thought of mine is about you know who,
The overwhelming sense of despair,
With no real way to repair,
Life is too complicated,
This is only going to be replicated.
Life goes on, and so do I,
In this now until the end of my time.

To my inner child

To my inner child within my soul,
I feel you, and cherish you,
Keep me sane, hold on to my humanity,
Remember the kindness and the compassion,
To always do what is right,
To always be honest with everyone and yourself,
Never let anyone take you away from me,
I love you, keep me sane.

If I die

If I die,
Be honest about me, I was human,
If I die,
Remember me for who I was and what I achieved,
If I die,
Don't mourn or grieve for me, I didn't like this,
If I die,
I want to have accomplished my dreams,
If I die,
Be good, and succeed in life, whatever you do,
Once I am dead,
Learn to love, excel and live more of a life, as I would have tried.

I am lonely

I am lonely,
The world has gone weird,
The atmosphere is cold, and the people are mutating,
Is anyone out there?
I am lonely,
This is getting out of control now,
Everything is going bad,
I can feel it, in my bones, and in my heart,
Maturity…
Realising as I progress and mature,
I become lonely, cutting people of
Making new friends and developing more skills,
I won't be lonely for long,
There are people out there who will be with me for life.

My walk through uncertainty

As I march through these times of uncertainty
I am reminded that my journey is also uncertain,
Unknown creatures beneath the surface, lurking in the shadows,
I know that whatever life throws at me, my resilience will keep me going,
Don't let the weight of the world crush you, or let any storms derail you,
Paths are choices in life, we choose ones that make us who we are,
Don't let people who don't know you cause more conflict,
There are many people in life who will love, and support throughout this,
For this journey I am on is only the beginning.
March to the beat of your own drums,
Stand with 10 toes to the ground,
Make a mark, have a lasting impact on this world,
This sad, and overly anxious world is not ready,
This is our year, MY YEAR,
Be good, me, love Harry

Ingram Content Group UK Ltd.
Milton Keynes UK
UKHW022236050723
424591UK00015B/574